Collection of poems

15 TO 30 ...

Be

COME

ING

A

Wo M an

Diane C. Anderson

Presented by: DANIA M. JOLLEY

15 to 30 … Be COME ING A WoMan!

Diane Christine Anderson

Presented by Dania M. Jolley

Published by Pecan Tree Publishing, August 2020

Hollywood, FL

www.pecantreebooks.com

978-1-7347430-6-7 Paperback

978-1-7347430-7-4 EBook

Library of Congress Control Number: 2020915338

Cover Design By: Dimitrinka Cvetkoski

Interior Design By: Dimitrinka Cvetkoski

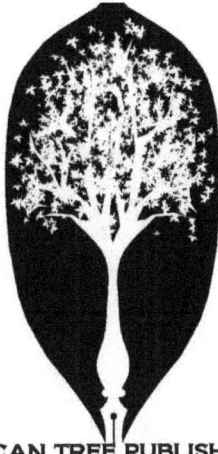

PECAN TREE PUBLISHING

Pecan Tree Publishing
www.pecantreebooks.com
Hollywood, Fl

Dedication

This book is dedicated to my mom, Diane Christine Anderson whose loving memory walks with me.

To all the women who have loved too much and loved too hard. To all those who have a love of the written and spoken word. To those who have written poems, songs or stories about love, heartache, and redemption – this work is dedicated to you.

And to my son, Kobe, his mere existence has taught me so much about joyous and unconditional love.

Acknowledgments

I would like to acknowledge and thank my Aunts Allysia Sneed and Wendy Harper for watching over me and being there for me since my mother's transition.

The Anderson family (Alfred, Lillie Mae, Alfred Jr and Barbara) who preceded my mom in death. And the Anderson grandchildren (Leon, Alante, Dorshica and Shavon) who carry the family legacy.

Girlfriends Brunch, a group of women who have become my sisters. Thank you for answering the call of sisterhood and always being in my corner; and for having the foresight to know what I need when I need it.

Thank you Pecan Tree Publishing for your guidance through the publishing process.

And to my mother's friends and past lovers, thank you for being on the journey with Diane as she was Be COME ING A WoMan!

Foreword

My big sister Diane was a dreamer and a woman of GOD. Diane was the type of woman whose beauty outwardly did not compare to the beauty inside. Brilliant and intelligent, it's no wonder she was dynamic with words. A portion of which you now hold in your hands.

I always admired her for many reasons. She was so pretty. She seemed so perfectly organized and always well put together. She was successful. And she did not hesitate to share that all that made Diane – Diane was due to her incredible faith in the Lord. I saw clearly that her personal example of faith, creativity, determination was a path to good success.

As a woman, she experienced love more than once. Love, as you will read in her words, sometimes did not rise to the standards she hoped for. Yet, Diane always approached relationships full of the hope for an everlasting love. She loved deeply, with loyalty and fierceness. Like me, she was always disappointed when love vanished. Her heart would break and mend within time and time again. Each farewell encouraged her to expect the man of her dreams. The one that would stay for always.

The love of her life, the one human that kept her aspiring was her daughter Dania Jolley. Diane regarded her as her greatest accomplishment. The Light she witnessed in Dania was a spiritual reminder of GOD and his divine power, creativity, and love. She witnessed her victory and success in her child and for that reason would always forge onward to the next good success, no matter what life threw at her.

Diane was a victorious woman; and she boldly declared it, "My name is victory in CHRIST JESUS. I always win in CHRIST JESUS. It is not over until I win in CHRIST JESUS." She believed in the power of words, and it is in her words here you will immerse in the power she was blessed with.

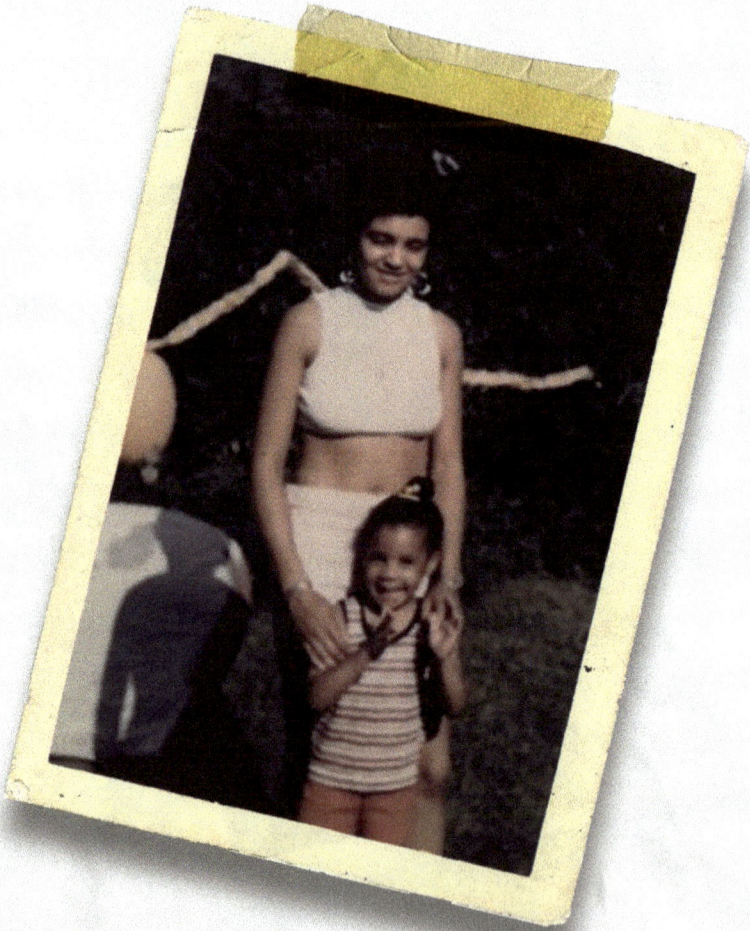

Invitation to My Mom's Words
By Dania M. Jolley

I have always needed help starting a story. Every paper, essay or story always started with a call to my mom. She was the educator, linguist, and mom. With her larger than life personality, she would always know the right words to use to capture the audience's attention. Today she is not here and I begin my story alone.

Alone is what my mom felt most of the time. She would tell me stories of feeling alone as a child, teen, and even as a young adult. She could be alone in a room full of people. This is when she would escape into a world of letters, words, and phrases. Armed with a pen and pad she was free to not be alone.

I believe a mother is a mythical being. She is the one who mysteriously appears and the one we believe to be immortal, until she is gone. When you lose a mom, it is beyond devastating. Your mom, my mom is the first person you know. She is your first friend and most times she knows you better than you know yourself.

Well, that is who Diane C. Anderson was to her family. She was ready for anything and fiercely protective of her family, time, and words. I remember when I was young, she would keep her poems in a binder next to the photo albums. I knew not to touch that binder. She is the one who would decide when she would share her poems with me. It was always a treat. She was awesome! Her flare for the dramatic would kick in as she would recite the poems to me. You could hear her innocence in "A Kiss", her joy in "My Little Girl" and her reverence in "King's Kid". As I got older, it was more of the same. I could not touch the poem book. She said I did not always put things back where they belonged, so my hands needed to stay off her treasure trove. Still, she enjoyed sharing them with me. It was always, "Dania, get the book and sit there." (I always knew what she meant). I smile thinking of those days.

In my mom's later years, we discussed her publishing the book (she had it copyrighted January 1982), and possibly turning it into a one-woman production (which she would produce). That is another dream I am determined to fulfill. My mom loved the theater. As a little girl, we would see all the Black theater productions when they came to town. My mom would save some money every month and at least twice a year we went to a big production. She absolutely loved the theater!

My mom had a stroke in 2016. As the tables turned and I became the caregiver, we really got busy plotting and planning the book launch and staging the play. Although we never got around to completing it before her passing, her wish was always to have the poetry book published. I believe her hesitation was the fact that these poems, these small works of literary art, were her innermost thoughts and feelings and she was not always comfortable being vulnerable. The poems in this book share my mom as a young girl learning of love; becoming a young woman experiencing heartache after heartache; transforming into a young mother exuding with joyous love for her child to the most blessed love of all, God's love!

It is true that Diane C. Anderson was a lover! She was a lover of people. She was a lover of words and how they fit together and flowed from the heart to paper. She was a lover of family. She was a lover of the Lord!

This book is divided into three chapters. Chapter 1 titled BEFORE; you will experience new love in poems like "A Kiss". In Chapter 2, titled RESURRECTION, you will experience sexual love in poems like "Release" to broken love in poems like "Child of the Blizzard". You will also see the healing of God's love. And, in Chapter 3 titled FREE, you will experience her love of words in poems like the one that bears the chapter's name.

I invite you to experience some of Diane's love through her words!

In Her Words...

15 to 30... Be COME ING A WoMan is a collection of poems reflecting the coming of age of a girl child to a sexual woman. The sadness and futility of a woman who had not been taught to love. Her life was shroud in fear and self-hate. From one relationship of failure to yet even more devastating attempts at failed relationships. Intimacy always looming as the dark abyss that would attack, and suck dry the very nature of the individual.

So many years spent guarding the small flame of hope within her soul. She didn't know that she had been touched by the Most High God at conception and that she would have to learn and achieve her mission through the byways and alleys of pain.

Today she stands strong and tall as a dedicated messenger of God's eternal love.

You may find yourself in this collection of poems. You may find your way of escape. You may bear the secret to cancelling your pain and filling yourself with joy.

Diane Christine Anderson

Collection of poems

by Diane Christine Anderson

15 TO 30...

Be COME ING

A

WoMan

Poems written from 1965 to 1980.

Contents

BEFORE
Intro

Do you remember your thoughts and feelings on love when you were 15-24? Do you remember that first kiss before womanhood?

We all have stories of that first love, that first kiss and that first heartache. That first time you became a "woman". My mom was a 15-year-old virgin, and with her first KISS she became a pregnant teen. My mom loss the baby girl hours after her birth. Tanya, would have been my older sister. My mom did not speak of her often but when she did you could feel the pain that loss left with her. My mom was always looking for love, some validation that she was worthy to be loved. Some patching for the loss of Tanya. Even through the pain - hiding and masking it - my mom always believed in a higher power, in God. She always came out of the pain, she never let it defeat her.

In those early years, the poems were written about past lovers about adoration, intimacy as well as, unhappiness and pain.

The poems in this chapter talk about those early ideas of LOVE, defining it and watching it transform you.

Take the journey and remember your first love.

before

A KISS

I cried with deep feelings.
It seemed my sobs would wreck the ceilings.

I cried like this all because of a kiss.
A kiss that to me meant love, which I thought was sent from
　　heaven above.

God had looked down and seen my sorrow.
And allowed me a lover to borrow.

To make him happy, I did thrive.
For I didn't know that I loved a jive.

With every girl, he did flirt.
And treated me as if I were dirt.

Finally, for him was gone the pain.
But the tears still came as rain.

Rain that falls and leaves the dew.
Tears that come when parted are two.

WAITING

You are a man, a beautiful man.
Tall, Black, Ambitious.
You have beautiful drive and aim for the sky.
Yet, While reaching for the sky, you overlook me.
It hurts.

You don't realize my feelings.
Deep so deep.
I feel from each fiber, vibration after vibration.
Reacting from my heart, hurting my mind.
I ache and yearn with needs.
Needs to be satisfied.

You realize, but you are ambitious.
Is it worth the pain?
If you were ever to love me,
The pain I feel now would be nothing.

LET'S JOIN

You are man.

I am woman.

We are two.

Here am I and

There are you.

Why can't the both join.

FOOLISH

Man asks.
Man desires.
But, man does not want.

Woman gives.
Woman pleases.
But woman does not receive.

What has become of affections, cares?
Do they exist anymore?
Or is man here only to see how many fools can be made.

A fool can be beautiful in her own way.
If the one she is foolish for accepts and appreciates.

But if she is forgotten her foolishness can hang like an
        albatross around her neck.
Tending to make her bow her head in shame.

If she believes what she has done was to please, even though
    rejected and can still walk with her head held high—-

Then she is a better woman than he a man.

    I AM SORRY.

LOVE

What is love?

Where does it begin?

Does it begin at all or maybe it is as God.

There with no beginning, no end.

Yet, always letting its presence be known.

CAN WE FORGET?

Life begins;
Love is shared;
Joys are known;
Pains instilled;
Times passes;
Wounds heal;
But do we ever forget?
Can we ever believe and be free to live again.
I am trying. Maybe death will tell.

TRANSFORMATION

I was once young. Now I am old.

I was once blind. Now I can see.

I once believed, Now I doubt.

I was once truthful. Now I lie.

How was I transformed?
Did I want to change?
Or did my world force me to become more a part of it?
To accept the phony glitter and lack of depth.
To bend to the demands of society and forsake
    my own inner demands.
I don't know how or when I was transformed.
But to you alone, Diane, I am sorry.

SOMETHING'S MISSING

What am I?
What do I want?
What leaves me empty?
Why is my soul so sad?
I feel as if something got away.
What?
I cry unto the night.
Something fill my emptiness.
Nothing comes.
I understand, I am alone.
But defeat I do not feel.
I have faith and I know fulfillment will come.

NOT FOR ME

Let me tell you of my love.
No, physical love you want no part of.
You have found Islam, Allah.
Understand our uniting can only be a praise to Allah.
The child the new life that may be created.
Understand I love Allah, but Islam is not for me.

A NEW BEGINNING

The touch
   Did he feel it?
It held something new.
Like a halo descending upon an angel's head.
Light shone all about.
And I felt my body quiver, with the thought-

   HE DOES CARE!

RESURRECTION
Intro

In her mid-20's now, my mom continued looking for love. She smoked a little weed, as you see in poems like "Wacky Weed". One story she told me was being at a party and getting high and dancing, she loved to dance. She was having a great time getting high until she heard the words of the song. What she heard was "...looking down the barrel of the devil's gun" and realized then that she needed to change how she was living her life. She stopped the drugs. Once my mom made up her mind, it was done. Her will was strong.

This chapter is full of poems about love, heartache and new found love. My mom had a lot of growth during this time. She was a single mother, navigating her way. Raised in a two-parent household this was new territory for her; however, she excelled. She started college and worked a full time job all while raising me. Now, today this is common for many women, however, in 1974 not so common. I enjoyed going to classes with my mom in the evenings and on the weekends. We were always together and became very close during this time, a bond that is unbreakable and will last to infinite and beyond. Poems like "My Little Girl" speak of our closeness. She graduated from DC Teacher's College (now UDC) and would start her career in education.

Also during his time, she had an intense love affair that would permeate her mind, body and soul. Len was a great guy. I liked him and was not aware of the anguish my mom went through when that love ended. As you can see from poems like "Ode to Len" and "Child of the Blizzard". As a kid, you think your parents are these beings, we forget they are women and men just like us. It was not until I had a couple of loves and heartaches of my own that I was really able to understand my mom's poetry.

This chapter ends powerfully as my mother found her way back to the church. I believe it was in 1978 that we started attending Rhema Christian Center. My mother loved the Lord with as much passion and intensity as she did past lovers. In poems like "A New You", you see life renewed through the eyes of a born again Christian.

Take the journey and experience more love, unconditional love and agape love!

THE MIND

Man! Pain! Illusion!

Why? I cry to the universe.
How? I look deep within myself.
When? What?
Yes! Again, the heart bleeds, the soul aches, the eyes flood,
 the mind
 the mind
 the mind
I can't express the mind.
The heart will cease to bleed.
The soul will exalt with the end of the ache.
The flood will dry.
But the mind will remember
 always
 always
 always
I must remember always, how the mind was fooled.
How the mind believed and rejoiced in the man, love.
And, now the mind must remember the man is gone, the love
was false.

Man! Pain! Illusion!

BENEATH THE SURFACE

We've touched the secrets of the universe together.
Yet can we not touch each other's hearts with enough
    trust that they may open with love as does a yielding
    water lily upon calm waters.
Looking on calm waters one cannot tell of the depth within.
Let us try and look deeper than the surface.
Into the innermost depths of the soul.
Fear protects the surface or should we say distorts the
    truth.
I can only speak of my fear.
I believe you care for me.
I feel it in your touch, see it in your eyes.
Yet my fears make me outwardly throw your cares to the
    wind.
Help me conquer my fear.
Help me believe in your love.
If it is real don't let us throw heed to the winds and lose
    something maybe too beautiful for this infested world.
I will try.
Try with me.

WACKY WEED

Let me befog my brain.

Let me cloud my eyes.

Let me slip beyond the realm of reality.

Let separate forms blend.

Let me wonder, will I return?

Allow me to trip!

HIGH

OPEN, OPEN, OPEN, OPEN

WIDER, WIDER, WIDER

FEEL, FEEL

my head explodes

I am HIGH!

RELEASE

Touch my hair, my head tingles.

Kiss my face, it radiates a smile.

Nibble my neck, sparks descend my body.

Caress my breast, the nipples harden.

Explore my womanhood, love seeps down my inner thighs.

Rub my legs, my knees are weak.

The feelings cause my toes to curl.

You have released me.

MY MAN

Many men have loved me
    But none as you.
Many have caressed my body
    You have embraced my mind.
Many have burdened my heart
    You have enlightened my soul.
Many have possessed my womanhood
    You have freed my spirit.
They were only my lovers
    You are truly my man.

ESSENCE

Your lips reach for mine
    The sea laps against the shore.
Your arms hold me
    The earth anchors the plant.
Your tongue explores my mouth
    The sun gives warmth.
I know I exist
    I have essence because of you.

A MESSAGE

Hold not to those things that have gone before.
Let not your mind dwell on that which is not happy.
For every sadness, exists a joy.
For every mistake, there is success.
Cultivate that which is of worth to you,
And allow to wane those things that appear vile.
As you evolve into self—fulfillment
Think not back on those you have left.
But cherish those who have followed.
And affluent amends will be yours.

EACH DAY

I will enjoy you for each day.
I offer no restraint for tomorrow.
I have no regrets for yesterday.
I want to know each bit of you.
I want to revel each of your vibrations.
I give you unadulterated affection.
I bestow my mind and soul for you to probe.
I entreat only that you receive what I invite.

ODE to LEN

Shall I begin with your marvelous, brilliant mind— full of thoughts, ideas, determination, dreams.

Or descend to your stable and uniformed feet— each toe joined to the whole, yet standing individual and independent.

Maybe I'll start with the center and allow my admiration of you to spiral encompassing each and every magnificent aspect of your total being.

The heart— is that my target. The heart that knows no malice, no greed, only an extending warmth for all in need.

The ears that listen so attentively to the woes of the world, bestowing no judgment, only offering sympathy.

The hands - unique, gentle in their exploring simplicity. Not demanding, inquiring in all they search and encounter.

Warm, soft, moist, yielding lips. Opening ever so slightly to allow and welcome the desire of another.

Eyes dark, piercing, understanding, forgiving, demanding, reprimanding, hypnotizing, enjoying. Eyes that fear not the yearnings of another's soul. Eyes that guard the desires of your own soul.

Yes, Len, all these things I see and receive from you. These are the reasons that I want to absorb your vibrations. Your beautiful existence requires my submission. I am grateful to whatever being thought me worthy to allow me to sun myself in your aura for just a little while.

LOVING

Love is as simple and complicated as
Everyday life.
Many have loved
Unsuccessfully, always hoping that
Eventually the right one will come.
Lonely people everywhere, hoping to find

Joy, before they die, and loving is
Over. Looking for that shared
Happiness, that changes
Nothingness into everything.
Surely believing that their missing part is
Only found in loving.
Never giving into despair.

LIGHTHOUSE

I want to be with you.
  Not against you.
I want to please you.
  Not deceive you.
I want to be pleased by you.
  Not appalled of you.

All beings are made to adapt.
I will shift and change accordingly.
No man stays forever the same.
Even as the solid rock chips and falls,
Water and wind give it a new shape.

I cannot extend my arm to the roaring lion,
No sooner than I can plant both feet in quicksand.

Who would be foolish enough to sow a seed in the snow,
Then hope it will embed itself in the soil and grow.

Who would wish on a falling star?

None without faith would do such things.

Yes, I sowed a seed in the snow
And so, did hope that it would grow.
I saw that falling star and prayed.

These and other things I did do because I wanted you.

But feelings must eventually give way to logic,
As logic is often conquered by feelings.

Where is the lighthouse?
I'm lost in a sea of emotions.
The storm is rising,
I am faltering.

Will I find my way?
I look to you.

CHILD OF THE BLIZZARD

Hey Brother-man, you asked for my number.
You called me.
You convinced me that making love with you was right.
And it was!
You guided my body and mind to the stars and floated me
    back.
You showed me how to feel and fill myself from head to toe.
You knocked at my heart's door.
You peeped through my windows of emotion.
I removed the barriers because I thought you were
    standing in a blizzard of loneliness.
I didn't want you to be cold.

Now, I seem to be the only one loving.
Were you a child of the blizzard, who came to bring me
unhappiness?
If so, please take it back.

The Conversation

Ring! Ring!

Lemuel:	"Still answering on the second ring."
Diane:	"Gives you time to change your mind."
Lemuel:	"No, it's habit."
Diane:	"Why did you give her so much attention?"
Lemuel:	"She was adjusting."
Diane:	"Why did you hinder his catering to me?"
Lemuel:	"I didn't care about that."
Diane:	"You showed a lack of respect for me."
Lemuel:	"I'm not going to cater to you."
Diane:	"I know. Keep all the pictures. I don't care."
Lemuel:	"Your jealousy goes too deep."
Diane:	"Are you going to keep all the pictures?"
Lemuel:	"Yes, they've been given to me."
Diane: (hesitantly)-	"Are you going to keep all the pictures?"
Lemuel	"Yes!"

Internally— I can't deal with this. It has got to stop.
He doesn't understand. He's crushing me.
(hang up the phone)
I can't. He won't call back.
Hang up the phone. No! I can't deal. Bang!

My soul is consumed with anger. Sleep, sleep heals and soothes all emotions. S-L-E-E-E-E-P!

By Diane Christine Anderson

NOT MY LEM

I met him
    He was tall, dark
But he's not my Lem.

I talked with him
    He spoke well
But he's not my Lem

He kissed me
    I accepted
But he's not my Lem.

He touched me
    His hands were smooth
But he's not my Lem.

I want my Lem.
I want to be in another place, another time.
I want to be where I can have my Lem and he have me.
And he and I can soar and become ecstatic in loving.

ACHE

1 want to yell, rant and rave.
I want to scream to the top of my voice.
I want to throw and bust furniture.
I want to tear this world apart.
I want to rid myself of this ache.
This dull, throbbing, continuous ache.
This ache that I know will go away and leave me void of
    the sweet memories of loving.

EMPTY

I feel like writing a poem
But I'm not sure what to write.
I could write how I ache without love.
Or how fulfilled I am with my man.
But I don't have a man.
And I don't really ache.

I feel EMPTY.

THE PILL

Do you know why I feel empty?
Do you really want to know?
I feel like the earth became barren.
Seeds are sowed in my body as the farmer sows his field.
But these seeds are not sowed to be fertilized.
They are only planted to die.
I wish they would catch and grow.
But that won't happen because I take the PILL.

MY LITTLE GIRL

There is a little girl in my house.
She's definitely not as quiet as a mouse.
She's full of fun and steam.
She reminds me of a sunbeam.
Her mind is open and alert.
Already she's learning to flirt.
She likes to read and stay near me.
We've been very close since she was three.
She's as fascinating as a dream,
And elegant as a queen.
She is my whole world because she is my little girl.

DANIA JOLLEY

Daughter of my heart
Always will I cherish your
Nearness and hope that you and
I will stay close forever.
Age and time will not cease the

Joy we share with each
Other, nor will we ever
Let our feelings and
Love falter.
Every day, I love you more than
Yesterday.

UNCOOL

How do I say I'm sorry when I've acted like a fool.

How do I take it back when I know I've been uncool.

How do I change the vibes when my actions have had no cause.

How do I make amends, Bill, or must I take the loss.

SUPERFICIALITY

If you want me call this number and I shall be manifested in the flesh to satisfy all your physical desires.

If your soul is in battle say, Diane, and I will chase the sorrow away and exalt your soul with pure unadulterated love.

If your spirit needs heightening, touch me and my spirit will mingle with yours to mitigate everyday living.

If none of these be your needs, then it has been ordained that I shall find my mate and lose him in superficiality.

FLIGHT

I imagine how an island feels.
Standing amidst the flowing waters.
Simply being the object to be played upon.
The waves rush in and slowly retreat.
Each time taking a bit of you with them.
Waves of flowing emotions.
Emotions that are free and flighty as the birds.
Landing only to pick the fruit from the out-thrusting
    arms of the tree.
Leaving nothing for the tree.
The tree gathers life gradually from the earth.
The earth gives willingly so the tree might live.
And the life of the tree gives the island its welcoming
    beauty.
And again, the waters rush in and slowly retreat.
As an army in battle, charge, fall back, regroup.
Constantly craving the reward of victory.
An unrealistic victory that only begins a cycle of charge,
    retreat.
I know how an island feels.
I have lived the giving of a tree.
I know that my loving has made someone's soul more beautiful.
Now I shall be the bird and take flight.

A NEW YOU

I've heard of your needs.
I've seen your desires.

Now let me introduce you to a friend.
One who is there from beginning to end.

One whose total existence evolved from love.
One sent to comfort from God above.

You've heard His name a thousand times.
I give Him to you because He's truly mine.

JESUS, the son of the living God.
He wants your mind; He wants your heart.

Ask Him in to guide your life.
Give up nothing, He's already made the sacrifice.

He loves you and wants to make you whole.
Give Him a chance, He'll renew your soul.

MANTLEPIECE

We do not know the mission of God.
We yield our earthly tabernacles as branches swaying
   in a strong, gentle wind.
Forces unseen bending and twisting us into perfection.
Perfection worthy to be set upon the King's mantle.
There are spaces for all upon the mantle.
The King is omni and enjoys all His creations.
Vessels of oak polished to the brilliancy of sun
   reflected streaks of gold.

FREE
Intro

My mom found freedom in the Lord. She was a new being in Christ.

About two years into teaching, she secured a full-time role as a Special Education teacher; some say she was exceptional at her job. Her student's adored her and she them. She wanted the best for the students who came to school; some under some horrible circumstances.. The students needed to acquire the necessary skills to be successful, but more importantly my mom saw that they needed love and someone to believe in them. She wrote "A Friend" during this time to remind everyone that we are all deserving of love and friendship.

My mom was always a dreamer and never gave up on love. She persisted to find that special one; however, the love that brought her the greatest joy was the love of God. His love was perfect. Poems like "King's Kid" and "My Place" (by the way, this is one of my favorite of her poems), spoke on her surrendering to God's awesome power and love.

My mom was finally FREE to be herself. Not looking for validation in love but enjoying love when it was there and waiting patiently until it came around again. Poems like "FREE" and "Dreamer" show the evolution of a young girl

You know with age comes a certain freedom. My mom ended this book of poems at the start of her thirties. There was more love, heartache, joy, discoveries, and poetry my mom has to share.

Thank you for taking the journey into her inner most feelings. I hope a poem or two touches you and you find some joy in knowing you are not alone on this journey called LIFE!

free

By Diane Christine Anderson

KING'S KID

Being a King's kid can be tricky.
But when Satan comes don't let him be frisky.
Command him in the name of the Lord,
To leave your abode and leave your soul.
How can you ever receive your rights.
With that fool running about.

The rights of a King's kid is total success.
To glorify God, everything must be best.
God's divine nature resides in you.
He promised to bless everything that you do.

If you don't believe Him, get out of the race.
If you want doubt, then God's kingdom is not your place.
Believe in the Saviour.
He died for you.
He'll crown you with glory and eternal life too.

I LOVE JESUS.

MY PLACE

In this world I've found my place.

I'll stand my ground and slack my pace.
I'll wait upon the Lord and exercise my faith.

Because I'm a King's kid.

I KNOW MY PLACE.

FREE

Poetry is whisperings of the soul.

We give ourselves to God, and He can make us whole.

His spirit has come to reside in me.

He taught me to love and made me free.

Now that I live in this eternal state.

I can ask your forgiveness and clean — wipe my slate

WRITER

I would like to be a writer and write flowery tales of
    love forever.
I want to be a writer.
    Writing progress, overcoming obstacles, treading on to
        the Promised Land.
I am a writer:
    I will write my story.

FRIEND

Hey little girl, why so blue!
    Don't your momma love you?
Hey little girl, you is shy!
    I dun tol' you 'bout the pie in the sky!
Cheer up that face and brighten dem eyes.
What I'm goin' tell you, gonna make you wise.

You is God's own creation.
Nobody else got your specifications.
Use what you got to climb that mountain.
Then share it with the world like a flowing fountain.

God dun gave you a real soft heart.
Don't let this world tear it apart.
Stretch out your arms and hug that child!
He's got a need raging wild.

Deep inside he needs to know, that somebody loves him,
    You show him so!
Rub his head and nudge him out.
Tell him this world ain't got room for doubt.
Urge him on until your end.

God sure made everyone at least one Friend.

…and on and on and on…

DREAMER

People look at her;
   wonderingly,
      "Why doesn't she worry?"
She's a dreamer.

   in wide eye astonishment,
      "Why doesn't she cry?"
She's a dreamer.

   with fierce resentment,
      "What does she dream?"
She smiles graciously and replies,

   "For your freedom."

WE ALL HAVE A STORY TO TELL

Before you leave these words that vividly paint the picture of a young girl BE COME ING a WoMan, think about your own story. What is your story?

Use this space to explore it in the way my poem did – in your own words.

What is your BEFORE?

What is your RESURRECTION?

What is your FREE?

The WoMan I am BE COME ING is ....

_____

_____

_____

_____

_____

_____

_____

_____

_____

_____

_____

_____

_____

_____

_____

_____

_____

_____

_____

_____

_____

_____

_____

_____

_____

_____

_____

_____

ABOUT THE AUTHOR

Diane Christine Anderson, mother, friend educator, poet, and Christian, was born and raised in Washington, DC. She was proud to be a native Washingtonian. She wrote poetry her whole life. This poetry book may be poems Diane wrote from 15 to 30, however, she continued writing poetry until her death. She wrote about LOVE, all areas of love, love of a man and woman, love of her daughter and the love of GOD. From A Kiss, written at 15 years old about a boy she was smitten with, to My Little Girl, written about the little girl she adored to My Place, written about her place in the Kingdom of GOD.

Diane, started her career in education in 1979 and devoted over 30 years to teaching in Special Education. Her students became an extension of her as she witnessed their successes from the small, like developing reading and writing skills to the big, like graduating and starting families. She gave her all to her students. Her devotion to her students' needs extended beyond the classroom and prompted her to start several nonprofits. Seeking Self Success 2, was focused on assisting people she meet in finding success within themselves. That non-profit morphed into Good Success Inc., where she would feed and clothe the homeless, making specials treats and baskets for them on those special holidays we may sometimes take for granted like, Mother's Day and Father's Day.

Her church home was Rhema Christian Center founded by her godparents, Bishop Calvin & Doris Givens. Through their love for Diane, they introduced her to the Lord and she never turned back. She believed her poetry, love of words and compassion where a gift from God and she never stopped writing and caring.

After Diane's passing, her daughter, Dania Michele Jolley, wanted to fulfill Diane's life-long wish to publish her poetry collection to share her love of words and her innermost feelings of love with the world.

www.ingramcontent.com/pod-product-compliance
Lightning Source LLC
Chambersburg PA
CBHW071101090426
42737CB00013B/2417